For Your Garden

HOT COLOR GARDENS

For Your Garden

HOT COLOR GARDENS

DARIA PRICE BOWMAN

FRIEDMAN/FAIRFAX
PUBLISHERS

A FRIEDMAN/FAIRFAX BOOK

© 1999 by Michael Friedman Publishing Group, Inc.

Library of Congress Cataloging-in-Publication Data available upon request

ISBN 1-56799-746-5

Editor: Susan Lauzau
Art Director: Jeff Batzli
Layout Designer: Meredith Miller
Photography Editor: Amy Talluto

Color separations by Fine Arts Repro House Co., Ltd.
Printed in Hong Kong by Midas Printing, Ltd.

1 3 5 7 9 10 8 6 4 2

For bulk purchases and special sales, please contact:
Friedman/Fairfax Publishers
Attention: Sales Department
15 West 26th Street
New York, NY 10010
212/685-6610 FAX 212/685-1307

Visit our website:
http://www.metrobooks.com

Table of Contents

INTRODUCTION

Themed gardens—whether loosely constructed around an abstract concept like contemplation or romance or specifically designed for a purpose like attracting butterflies or pleasing children—are enormously appealing. And all-of-a-color gardens, most notably white or blue gardens, have more than a few admirers.

The hot color garden—one that claims its character from vivid colors such as red, orange, yellow, gold, and magenta—may not suit everyone's tastes. But for those who relish bright colors, strong contrasts, and visually demanding combinations, the hot color garden is a rewarding sight.

This is not a timid color scheme, and it's not one for every garden—or for every gardener. But for people who love the simmering shades of bright tones, the hot color garden is an exciting, vibrant place that delights the senses and fires the imagination. Hot colors bring to mind the embers of a campfire or the roaring flames of a fire gone out of control. These are the colors of sunrise and sunset. Of ripe fruit and tropical birds. Of south-of-the-border beaches and exotic marketplaces. Of children's scribbled drawings and 1960s fashion designers.

Though left to her own devices nature rarely errs in creating color combinations, we who manipulate her elements have been known to invent less-than-worthy color schemes in our overenthusiastic efforts. Many of these mistakes have been made using colors that are simply incompatible; chartreuse ladys' mantle and lemon yellow 'Hyperion' daylily, for example, can create a rather bilious effect. Yet with the right formula, fiery shades of reds and yellows and their derivatives become compelling color statements.

In the photographs on the following pages we will wander through gardens whose creators have tamed nature's sizzling products. We'll look at the range of hot colors and how they combine with other colors, purple with yellow, for example, or red with orange. And we'll immerse ourselves in the steamy, sometimes overheated, but stunningly beautiful realm of the hot color garden.

OPPOSITE: Extensive gardens surrounding an Oregon homestead are ablaze with orange, yellow, pink, and white dahlias. The rounded dahlias bloom in marked contrast to the carmine exclamation points of cardinal flower (*Lobelia cardinalis*). Gardens with such a riot of color run the risk of appearing chaotic unless they have some unifying theme. Here, the repetition of form in the shape of dahlia flowers, along with a clever spacing of the lobelia spikes, prevents this vivid garden from spinning out of control.

ABOVE: Pink, a marvelously versatile color, results from the combination of red with white. But consider the striking difference between a pastel pink bloom and the vivid hot pink petals of *Cineraria multiflora* pictured here. Pink flowers change their character, too, depending on their companions. Hot pink becomes more restrained when partnered with paler versions of its own shade. It will seem to simmer when planted among deep purples and rich blues. And when orange and dark red are introduced, the atmosphere becomes decidedly heated.

ABOVE: Nature's affinity with modern art is no better demonstrated than in this close-up portrait of a red-on-yellow variety of *Gazania splendens*. Vividly patterned flower forms like this one make a powerful design statement, but also make it difficult to combine the blooms effectively with other plants. Some suitable companions for this *Gazania* might include marigolds, daylilies, goldenrod, or dahlias in the same shade of gold, as well as red lobelia or celosia.

OPPOSITE: A mass planting of 'French Mixed' marigolds in shades of gold, orange, and umber demonstrates the power of a simple design scheme. The marigold, among the most unpretentious of annual flowers, achieves such a strong visual impact because of the intensity of its colors. The vignette is further empowered by the repetition of the plant's uncomplicated form.

BELOW: Though blood-red Flanders poppies appear only briefly and the foliage yellows and dies soon after the flowers fade, this poppy is valued in the hot color garden for its potent color. The velvety petals appear all the redder beside the snow white tubular blooms of flowering tobacco (*Nicotiana alata*).

ABOVE: While the daffodil is the patriarch of the spring garden, the tulip is the reigning queen. And red tulips are arguably the most regal. Top-selling varieties include 'Appledoorn', 'Red Emperor', 'Red Riding Hood', 'Red Shine', 'Red Leader', 'Baston', 'Hollandia', and 'Cheerleader'.

ABOVE: Holiday hothouse favorites, amaryllis can be found outdoors in tropical settings. But here a pair, each boasting a multitude of orange-red blooms, are firmly upstaging the more delicate yellow spurs of a stand of columbines (*Aquilegia* spp.) in a temperate setting. Hot color gardens frequently employ the classic combination of reds and yellows. The key is in carefully selecting the exact shades of these colors that will create a pleasing palette.

ABOVE: The palette of this thickly planted mixed border includes strong color statements with the juxtaposition of rich wine and burgundy adjoining yellows and golds. The splotches of bright red in the form of summer-blooming montebretia (*Crocosmia* spp.) and lilies keeps the overall temperature on the high side. Goldenrod (*Solidago* spp.) and *Ligustrum* gleam gold along the slope.

RIGHT: Majestic patriarch of the daffodil clan, the 'King Alfred' cultivar pictured here seems to define spring with its jaunty yellow trumpets. 'Dutch Master' is another reliable, large-flowering variety. Daffodils add hot color at what can be a particularly cold time of year, and their diversity of form and range of shades make daffs not only useful, but perhaps essential in the spring garden. In addition to the most typical varieties, there are miniatures like 'February Gold' and 'Tete a Tete' and orange-accented versions, including 'Kissproof', 'Tahiti', 'Wild Carnival', and 'Ambergate', from which to choose.

BELOW: Perfectly formed floribunda roses are among the gardener's most elusive achievements, as most roses require vigilant care. But attentive gardeners will be rewarded by the exquisite beauty of this royal member of the plant kingdom. Renowned yellow and gold rose varieties include the bright 'Gold Bunny', pictured here, along with 'Graham Thomas', 'Golden Showers', 'Mountbatten', 'Limelight', and 'Marechal Niel'.

ABOVE: A skilled hand is required in order to successfully combine the tones of magenta-pink, as represented in this 'Raspberry Rose' impatiens, with other strong colors. The simplest route is to take on other shades of pink, as well as reds leaning toward blue and purple. These combinations have a pleasing shimmering quality. Far less likely to succeed is the combination of magenta with oranges and golds, though there are gardeners who create colorful masterpieces while breaking all the "rules."

OPPOSITE: Old-fashioned rose campion (*Lychnis coronaria*) brings not only the brilliance of its diminutive magenta blooms, but also the soft sensuousness of its downy silver foliage to the border or garden bed. Silver leaves, including those of artemisia, yarrow, helichrysum, lavender, catmint, santolina, lamb's ears, and some thyme varieties, serve to intensify hot colors, soften discordant color combinations, and create visual "rest stops" between and among vivid plantings. The same role is often played by white blooms, softly variegated foliage, and swaths of green.

ABOVE: The sizzling beauty of a multihued lily is only slightly cooled by a summer shower. Oriental, Asiatic, trumpet, and tiger lilies, all of which grow from bulbs, make exciting accents in perennial beds and borders. Among the most notable hot color varieties are 'Citronella', a bright lemon yellow with dark spots; 'Fire King', an orange-red tiger lily type; a Turk's cap lily, also known as 'Tenuifolium', which is brilliant red; and *Lilium hansonii*, an orange-red lily that grows up to 5 feet (1.5m) tall.

OPPOSITE: A patch of brilliant orange celosia creates a glowing sweep of color through a wide summer border. Vivid spikes of purple salvia form another band of a more tempered color behind, keeping the fire of the orange flames from leaping out of control, while burnt orange and yellow dahlias spice up the left side of the border.

Chapter One

HOT COLOR PLANTINGS

A new bed or border is to a gardener what a blank canvas is to an artist. With each plant, the gardener fills a space with a personal expression of color, texture, and form much the way an artist creates a painting with strokes or dabs of paint. No two gardens are exactly alike because the people who plant them are individuals with their own set of ideas, prejudices, experiences, and desires. And because nature has her quirks and idiosyncrasies, a plant in one bed will behave and appear differently when grown in another set of conditions.

Some gardens evolve through happenstance and serendipity, while others are the product of a painstaking design process, with careful attention paid to every detail. The success of the resulting garden does not depend on the gardener's training or level of expertise—rather, what seems to matter most is the creator's inspiration. Try your own combinations of hot colors, using your imagination and the harmonies found in nature for inspiration and taking your cue from the beds and borders in this chapter.

Everywhere there are gardens—from modest backyard beds to elaborate estates—the vision that becomes a garden is ultimately a gift to us all. On the following pages are some of those gifts given by gardeners whose vision incorporates nature's most brilliant colors, whose inspiration is fired by horticulture's steamy side.

OPPOSITE: Red, yellow, and hot pink zinnias stretch along a simple garden path, attracting the attention of hummingbirds and butterflies. Zinnia hybrids are offered in a kaleidoscope of color, with some seed companies featuring as many as twenty-five varieties ranging from single, daisylike blooms to dahlia-flowered types. Colors include yellow, gold, peach, orange, salmon, pink, rose, cherry, scarlet, and white.

ABOVE: Annual flowers like these 'Disco Flame' marigolds have served as the mainstay for generations of hot color garden aficionados. Along with marigolds in all their forms, zinnias, salvia, celosia, geraniums, and begonias have long been the traditional favorites. Today's gardeners, though, have far more choices than their predecessors did. Every year plant developers and hybridizers create new cultivars that tease us from the pages of catalogs.

ABOVE: At his garden at Giverny, the painter Claude Monet filled a long arbor-covered allée with orange, yellow, and red nasturtiums. By summer's end, the nasturtiums escaped from the confines of the narrow beds and sprawled along the gravel path. The gardeners at Giverny continue to plant nasturtiums following Monet's design, and cottage gardeners everywhere follow his lead, filling window boxes and pots with these delightful blooms.

OPPOSITE: Hot-toned tulips in a lively pageant march through a wide bed, where they have been artfully arranged in swaths of bold red, lemony yellow, and extravagant bicolors. Tulips in any color scheme look their best when planted en masse.

ABOVE: Gold, with a smattering of russet, tumbles along the length of a narrow bed. This vivid display relies on only two plants—'Early Sunrise' tickseed (*Coreopsis* spp.) and blanket flower (*Gaillardia* spp.)—for enormous visual impact. Using large quantities of a limited number of plants will result in a certain amount of "down time," when the bed will be without color, even with the most reliable long-bloomers. On large properties, gardeners will look to other beds to provide visual interest before and after a big performance like this one.

ABOVE: A late summer border explodes with fiery bloom. Goldenrod, montebretia (*Crocosmia* spp.), *Ligularia*, yarrow, and tickseed are aflame in shades of yellow, orange, gold, and red. A scattering of white flowers and strong foliage support keep the garden from burning out of control.

ABOVE: An Impressionist painter might approach this pretty scene with dabs of red paint to indicate the cluster of orange-red dahlias in the foreground, with a subtle repetition of red for the roses at the rear. Here and there, the artist would add hints of yellow to suggest the yarrow and hollyhocks that fill the middle ground. Note how this artistic gardener has matched the verdigris armillary with blue-green dahlia leaves.

LEFT: In a lush bed, large stands of perennials have been arranged with considerable attention to shape and height, as well as to color. Pink and yellow hollyhocks form a towering backdrop for clusters of bright lavender mallows, lipstick-red sprays of montebretia (*Crocosmia* spp.) and jaunty disks of yellow *Rudbeckia*. Though the overall effect is unfeigned and naturalistic, the selection of plant material is far from arbitrary.

ABOVE: Blocks of annuals form a crazy quilt of vivid colors in a wide garden bed. Verbena in a rainbow of hot colors mounds softly beneath flowering tobacco in hot pink and white. In a long garden bed, you might take this effect to the next level, borrowing from the legendary colorist Gertrude Jekyll. Imagine a garden bed that begins with plants in cool tones of pink, purple, blue, and white and progresses to a warmer palette of pinks, purples, and reds. The colors increase in intensity with more reds along with yellows and ultimately orange, only to cool off toward the far end of the border.

ABOVE: Clusters of gold lilies stand in stark contrast against a background of hot pink. Gardeners planning a bed or border find that such bold contrasts can quickly become overwhelming when done with a heavy hand. But when used artfully in limited scope, unexpected contrasts make a garden bed come alive with visual interest.

OPPOSITE: A field of bright yellow poppies seems to soak up the sun and radiate its warmth. Masses of a single type of flower makes a powerful statement. And when long-blooming varieties are used, the effect is truly breathtaking.

ABOVE LEFT: Sweet William (*Dianthus barbatus*) is an early-summer-blooming plant that introduces a gay palette of pink, red, and wine to garden beds. Delightfully versatile, sweet William will blend with cooler pale tones when needed, but this biennial is just as adept at turning up the heat when accompanied by warm shades of red, crimson, magenta, scarlet, hot pink, and burgundy.

ABOVE RIGHT: Viewed casually, this bloom looks simply like a red rose—in this case a groundcover variety known as 'Chilterns'. But a true colorist will see far more. There are hints of hot pink that come from the reflection of strong sunlight. Specks of strong golden-yellow light up the center of a full-blown bloom while emitting white-hot licks of flame. Train yourself to discern the subtle gradations of color within each flower, and you will begin to see surprising possibilities for color combinations in the garden.

OPPOSITE: Once scorned by sophisticated garden designers as ordinary and old-fashioned, the coleus has made a remarkable comeback in horticultural circles. The mixed-variety display pictured here shows some of this useful plant's range of color and pattern. Hot pinks edged with pistachio green, rich burgundy with a ribbon of chartreuse along the margin, and deep maroon with just a hint of light green are only a few examples. Coleus thrives in the shade and is equally at home in garden beds or in pots.

ABOVE: Smooth magenta disks of rose campion (*Lychnis coronaria*) bloom against the nubbly texture of sulfur yellow yarrow (*Achillea filipendula*), producing a truly arresting combination. Mixing different textures and flower forms is another way to introduce excitement, both visual and tactile, into your garden.

LEFT: The perky face of this multicolored pansy stands alone among bright yellow peers. Pansies are nearly ubiquitous in spring gardens in northern climates, and are favorite winter-time plants in warmer zones. Their colors range from icy white to cool sherbets to much warmer shades of rose, orange, and yellow. Pansies are at their best when planted in a monochromatic scheme or as a jaunty color mix.

OPPOSITE: A young smoke bush (*Cotinus coggygria*) merely hints at its future role in a border that is currently dominated by a sprawling patch of tickseed (*Coreopsis tinctoria*). At maturity, the smoke bush can reach more than 10 feet (3m) in height and may nearly equal that in width. With its strong burgundy color and pleasing form, the smoke bush is often called upon to serve as an anchor in the hot color border.

Chapter Two

WORKING TOGETHER: COMBINING HOT HUES WITH OTHER COLORS

The way we see and experience color is a complex relationship of science—the physical properties of light and sight—and of psychology—how we perceive these physical realities based on our training, personality, and experience. This is why we cannot be quite sure what someone else means when he or she speaks of magenta or ivory or burnt umber.

To better understand the use of color in the garden, it is helpful to work with the color wheel. Visualize a pie that has been sliced into six pieces that represent the three primary colors—blue, yellow, and red—and three secondary colors—green, purple, and orange. On the standard color wheel, orange is placed between red and yellow, because it is a blend of those two primary colors. Green stands between blue and yellow and purple is flanked by blue and red.

Complementary colors are those opposite each other on the color wheel—thus purple and yellow are complementary, as are orange and blue, and green and red. Harmonious color combinations make use of colors that are adjacent to one another—red and purple; blue and green; yellow and orange; and orange and red. Contrasts are created when colors do not share a color connection—red with blue, for example, or yellow with blue. The particular shade, tone, or tint of a color may have a great deal to do with whether or not it makes a good combination with another color, so you must trust your eye and not simply rely on traditional wisdom about what makes a favorable color combination.

And while the science of color is helpful in designing pleasing color combinations, intuition, character, wit, whimsy, and a sense of personal style—in other words, non-scientific, highly idiosyncratic elements—play an equally important role. In the following pages we will explore how art and science work together creatively in the hands of the hot color gardener.

ABOVE: Though the colors are brilliant, there is an ethereal, delicate quality to this meadow garden, where scarlet poppies and pale blue flax predominate. Such a lighthearted effect might also be achieved with *Lobelia cardinalis* and bachelor buttons; pink and blue larkspur; verbascum and coreopsis; Russian sage and cosmos; or *Celosia spicata* and *Ipomopsis.*

OPPOSITE: An impressionistic blur of color is created with free-flowering yellow marigolds, burgundy and pink petunias, and purple lobelia. The gardener has invented a marvelous set of complementary, contrasting, and harmonious color combinations with a limited number of plants. The fact that all of these plants are about the same height offers a calming and unifying influence. The streak of frothy white alyssum at the edge seems to hold back the tide of color.

ABOVE: The juxtaposition of purple and yellow is among the most exciting of color combinations, a fact that can be explained by their opposing positions on the color wheel. These are known by colorists as complementary colors. Here, marigolds, petunias, and geraniums contribute their luscious tones.

OPPOSITE: One sure way to combine hot colors with other color ranges is to mix various hues of a single type of plant. The jewellike tones of spring primroses (*Primula* spp.) are clear and intense. The purple blooms complement the buttery yellow flowers, but also have a built-in complementary note with their own yellow centers. The orange-red type is an example of how color harmony works. And the pink, which is a pale form of red, shows us the beauty of contrasts. White primroses seem to intensify all the other color relationships, while the highly textured green leaves are a unifying force. The massed planting approach makes this multicolored display especially potent.

ABOVE: An explosion of rhododendron and azalea blooms provides a clear demonstration of how color rules are made to be broken. Do the mauve, pink, and coral tones relate happily with the nearby yellow and orange flowers? To some eyes, it is a spectacular association; to others it's less than comfortable. The airy, tumbling, and naturalistic form of these shrubs makes such highly charged color combinations far easier for the eye to accept than plantings that appear more contrived.

OPPOSITE: Hot colors surge throughout this delightfully appealing cottage garden, where color rules don't seem to matter. Who would think that frilly pink poppies and magenta rose campion would look so good next to bicolored gloriosa daisies? But there is no doubt that these unexpected combinations are completely charming.

ABOVE: A confident gardener has created a highly stylized garden using three elements—boxwood, santolina, and marigolds—in a design that may have taken its inspiration from Victorian bedding gardens. But the effect here is stunningly contemporary and idiosyncratic. Note the way in which the sunny marigolds highlight the almost-hidden flowers of the santolina and the yellow-green new leaves of the boxwood.

LEFT: In a garden where space is limited, it is essential to make use of vertical areas. Here, a tower of plant baskets barely contains a bountiful cascade of blooms. While sunshiny yellow is the predominant color, there are patches of red and several shades of pink scattered throughout. Variegated foliage also makes an appearance in each tier of the flower tower.

OPPOSITE: Early summer colors frequently seem softer and less heated than the hues of later months, a function, in part, of the sun's intensity. In a cheerful garden vignette, glowing orange-red poppies bow before a bowl of fresh strawberries, while the last few blooms of rosy foxgloves crane their necks above.

ABOVE: Dahlias, which are tender plants that grow from fleshy tubers, produce some of the most vivid stars of the hot color garden. 'Vectra' dahlia is a gold mum type with orange shadings on the tips of its many petals. 'Contraste' has wine red blooms that fade to white at the ends of the petals. There are perfectly rounded pompon varieties and spidery star types, as well as fringed, double, and single cultivars. Dahlia colors range from innumerable red tones like wine, scarlet, magenta, crimson, rose, and pink to every shade of orange and yellow imaginable. Of course, there are pastels and whites, and a full menu of bicolors and shaded varieties from which to choose.

OPPOSITE: Clusters of glowing orange lilies become the focal point in a corner of a hot color garden in mid-July. Surrounding blooms in shades of light purple, brilliant red, and delicate yellow flutter about the leading players as if they were a well-dressed cast of extras in a Broadway musical. Choosing a star and letting the contrasting-colored plants act in supporting roles is a well-loved method of combining different color ranges.

ABOVE: Here, the spirited combination of oranges, reds, purple, and white are linked by the relaxed forms of most of the plants. A dissonant note comes from the beautiful white lilies at the back of the border; their demeanor is notice-ably formal in comparison with their sprawling neighbors.

OPPOSITE: It would be difficult to imagine a more elegant sight than this foundation border with a silver and red theme. Here, red 'Sarabande' roses stand guard over a series of silver mounds of lambs ears, artemisia, and *Convolvulus cneorum*.

ABOVE: Pink dianthus and crimson peonies make delightful early-summer plant partners. Pairing plants in different shades of the same color family is one way to make sure your colors harmonize. If grouped with a few pastel or white-bloomed neighbors, this corner of the garden would take on a far cooler personality. With the addition of more red, some hot pink tones, and perhaps a bit of purple, it would truly begin to simmer.

OPPOSITE: In a corner of an unpretentious country garden, a collection of plants forms a hodgepodge of warm color and interesting shapes. Spiky snapdragons in citrusy colors join masses of frothy pink roses and geraniums. Note the wealth of green in this scheme, which helps relieve the relentless color. There are times when an uncalculated, easy approach to plant combinations results in a lovely and inviting display.

Chapter Three

ALL-OF-A-COLOR GARDENS

While the idea of creating a single-color garden appears to be simple enough, doing it well requires considerable skill. Working with hot colors has its own set of difficulties, too, so when we encounter an especially beautiful monochromatic display in shades of orange, red, or yellow, we are quite likely seeing the work of a master gardener.

To achieve success with a monochromatic palette, attention must be paid to the depths of color. These gradations are usually described as hue, value, and intensity. Hue is essentially pure color without any pigments of other colors and with no hint of white, black, or gray. The value of a color is the way colorists describe how light or dark a color is in its relationship with white or black. Colors with a lighter value are described as tints of a color, while those that lean toward black are known as shades.

Once we allow ourselves to appreciate the complexity of color, we will never again see simply red geraniums or green grass. Instead, we will notice the touch of blue in the geranium's bud and marvel at the luminosity of the verdant blades as we watch them glisten with raindrops.

On the next few pages, we are permitted a glimpse at the results of a number of color experiments in gardens where the intricacies of hue, shade, and tone are thoroughly understood.

OPPOSITE: Plants in pots give the gardener an enormous range of opportunities to experiment with color. Here, containers of geraniums form a zigzagging swath of heated red through dense plantings. With the simple step of replacing three pots of geraniums with, for example, more pink dianthus or purple *Agapanthus*, which are already represented in this vignette, the character of the garden can be dramatically altered.

ABOVE: A clever combination of painted daisies (*Chrysanthemum coccineum*) in shades of pink exhibits a painterly approach to a monochromatic design. Note the way the bright yellow centers of the painted daisies serve to unify the planting combination. By employing only one plant species in a variety of shades, you can create an impressionistic display that is enormously pleasing. Plants to use this way include sweet William, asters, daylilies, lupines, irises, peonies, astilbes, tulips, daffodils, and tender plants like petunias, marigolds, flowering tobacco, begonias, geraniums, and gazanias.

ABOVE: In a deep border, a gardener has created an explosion of rich reds using petunias, flowering tobacco (*Nicotiana alata*), sedum, dahlias, amaranth, and snapdragons (*Antirrhinum* spp.). The reds range from ruby to deep cinnamon, providing a spectrum of color within the same family. Another key to this appealing mixture is the number of varying shapes and textures, from the starry tobacco flowers to the frilly petunia petals to the flat umbels of sedum to the downy plumes of amaranth.

OPPOSITE: In this vignette, petunias and verbena form a floral carpet of cherry red. When taking a monochromatic approach, it is possible to create wondrous color harmonies with only a few types of plants because hybridizers have taken nature's colors to extraordinary lengths, now offering a remarkable wealth of hues, shades, and tints.

ABOVE: Vivid yellow predominates in this traditional English border. Among the standout plants are 'Chandelier' lupines, 'Sungleam' delphiniums, garden loosestrife (*Lysimachia punctata*), and 'Firecracker' loose-strife. Yellow is one of the hues that includes tones from hot to cool, and this garden shows off nearly the entire range. An abundance of frothy white, paler yellows, and rich foliage serve to create a personality that is more mellow than ardent.

OPPOSITE: Mounds of marigolds carpet the front of a long border. The simplest way to achieve a harmonious effect in the hot color garden is to fill it with varieties of the same species. Here, compact hills of 'Aurora Fire' (front left) and large mophead marigolds lead to an inspiring drift of 'Lemon Gem'.

ABOVE: A brick wall makes the ideal support for a harmonious monochromatic palette of oranges. 'Ellen Houston' dahlias, assertive nasturtiums, and montebretia (*Crocosmia* spp.) create layers of color as they retreat toward and then climb the wall. Silky roses accent the red end of the range, while dark foliage intensifies the simmering color scheme.

OPPOSITE: This charming front garden greets visitors with its vivid red and yellow display. Wine-colored foliage of barberry (*Berberis* spp.) and vibrant dahlias and roses keep the scene firmly anchored, while red-hot poker and other orangey accents make important contributions. Blue-green foliage here and there intensifies the power of the reds.

ABOVE: When red is mixed with blue, purple is the result. The addition of yellow to red, on the other hand, produces orange. The key to creating the kind of pleasing single-color display found in this sizzling sprawl of petunias, flowering tobacco (*Nicotiana alata*), and verbena is to use colors with the same inclinations. The red tones and shades here share a tendency toward the blue end of the spectrum as opposed to reds with a closer relationship to yellow.

LEFT: Massive rhododendrons and majestic azaleas play the leading roles in a luxuriant spring garden bordering a small driveway. Hot pinks and reds are tempered somewhat by paler shades of pink and by the white candytuft (*Iberis* spp.) that clings to the rocky slope. Most varieties of evergreen rhododendrons and azaleas, which are kissing cousins, botanically speaking, feature blooms in shades of pink, mauve, red, purple, and white. Deciduous azaleas, especially the delightful Exbury strains, are known for their fiery reds, oranges, and yellows.

ABOVE: A pretty spring display is not so much sultry as it is warm and inviting. Clear yellow is a chameleon of a color, changing its personality depending on its proximity to hot or cool colors. Cheery yellow tulips mix with old-fashioned cowslips (*Primula veris*) and parchment-colored hellebores in an exuberant greeting of spring.

ABOVE: Sunny yellow marigolds (*Tagetes erecta*) and single-flowered dahlias in a nearly identical shade glow warmly in a corner of the garden. Because the flower forms of these two plants differ dramatically—the marigolds form dense, nearly fuzzy globes while the daisylike dahlia's distinct petals have sharp, clean lines—the combination remains dynamic and interesting. When designing a monochromatic garden, take care to add variety in shape, texture, height, and growth habit.

OPPOSITE: 'Prima Donna' daylilies, Peruvian lilies (*Alstroemeria* spp.), threadleaf coreopsis, and California poppies are included in a lushly planted corner of a walled garden bright with shades of gold and orange. Instead of the intensity of a red theme, these tones betray a more light-hearted ambiance.

ABOVE: Evocative of the south of France and other sun-drenched spots, fiery red geraniums and begonias tumble onto the pavement and sprawl from pots hung on a wall, proving that even a small courtyard or terrace can be home to a stunning hot color display. The simplicity of this monochromatic arrangement contributes to its success. Though white is often used to temper the fervor of hot colors in the garden, here the white-washed facade of the house actually seems to intensify the heat.

OPPOSITE: Because of their unique spirelike form and vivid brick red color, these lupines demand attention. More subtle, but still wanting to be noticed, is the large clump of red fuchsia below the stone figure. This repetition of color is a design mechanism used to encourage the eye to travel from one space to another, without creating competition between the two elements. If the gardener had substituted a vivid yellow plant for the fuchsia, the viewer's attention would be lured back and forth in response to an uneasy volley of visual signals.

Chapter Four

HOT COLORS IN CONTAINERS

*H*umans have been growing plants in pots since ancient times—terra-cotta pots used for gardening date to at least 2100 BC. No doubt the effort was strictly utilitarian in its early days, but the use of decorative pots, as well as the practice of ornamental horticulture, grew out of our human need to beautify our surroundings.

Today's gardeners can choose among an almost overwhelming variety of containers in which to grow plants. From basic terracotta to ornate cast iron to dramatic stone and easy-care fiberglass, pots and containers expand the garden's possibilities.

Patios and terraces, balconies and windowsills, paved dooryards and driveways are made more beautiful with well-planted pots. Tropical and tender species can be stored indoors when the weather becomes too cool for their safety. Spaces too small or lacking in suitable soil for beds and borders are enlivened with the color and scent of tubs and urns filled with annuals.

The use of potted plants also gives the gardener the opportunity to experiment easily with color combinations. Moving a pot of bright yellow marigolds, for example, to a spot with purple plantings will create a far different effect than if it is placed among reds and oranges. You can actually change the garden's personality in a matter of minutes by merely moving a few containers!

In this chapter we'll see how some highly skilled and very individual thinkers have used potted plants to prove that no two gardens will ever look alike.

ABOVE: A large glazed pot is resplendent with a monochromatic assemblage of red geraniums, yellow marigolds, and orange-red single dahlias with brilliant yellow centers. A sure spirit-lifter, this planter is best placed in a dooryard or along a well-traveled path, where it will brighten the day of all who pass by.

OPPOSITE: In a highly stylized composition, pots of marigolds, gazania, California poppies, felicia, pansies, and petunias compete for attention amid a myriad of elements. Composed primarily of yellows, accents of orange in the form of marigold petals and nasturtium flowers add more heat to the design, while purple pansies and other violet-hued flowers cool things off a bit.

ABOVE LEFT: A terra-cotta chimney pot is all but obscured in a froth of sulphur yellow blooms of dwarf broom (*Genista lydia*). Gardeners who make extensive use of containers, and who have the luxury of storage space for specimens not yet in bloom, can arrange a steady parade of exciting performers throughout the season. One might begin with daffodils and tulips, continue with Oriental lilies, follow with hydrangeas, and finish up with mums. Once the blooms have faded, the plants are removed to the staging area to make room for the next act.

ABOVE RIGHT: Perched somewhat precariously on the corner of a deck railing, a delicately fluted terra-cotta pot cradles a few brilliant 'Mansella' yellow double tulips brushed with subtle red streaks. Many gardeners enjoy forcing bulbs in order to have blooms in the dead of winter, rather than having to wait until spring. The key to success in forcing bulbs is fooling them into "thinking" they have spent the winter in very cold conditions. This trick can actually be achieved by storing bulbs in the refrigerator before planting them.

OPPOSITE: With a prolific flowering habit that produces masses of yellow-to-orange-to-hot pink blooms, the shrub verbena (*Lantana camara*)—shown here in standard form—is a one-plant, multihued hot color garden. Here, the shrub verbena is attractively mixed with pots of black-eyed Susans and a mixed container of dahlias, strawflowers, and vinca vine. A perfect planting for a sunny deck.

ABOVE LEFT: Sometimes one container provides all the hot color you need—this hanging basket of 'Hot Pink' petunias is unusually full and lush. Petunia hybridizers have made great strides in improving the species, and have actually developed some varieties that do not require regular deadheading. Some new petunias combine the large size of grandiflora types with the free-flowering habit of the multifloras, and there are heavily ruffled and double varieties from which to choose. Petunias contribute rich pink, mauve, purple, scarlet, magenta, red, and rose colors, and a few pale yellows. Can an orange variety be far away?

ABOVE RIGHT: An abundance of lipstick red geraniums cascades from hanging baskets, tumbles from windowsills, and overflows door-side pots in an exuberant scene. Brilliant blue shutters along with a scattering of white geraniums make effective visual anchors here.

OPPOSITE: A trough-shaped box brims with geraniums outside a quaint French farmhouse, while other plantings—including a narrow border and plenty of hanging pots—add interest at every level. The jewellike reds are accented by pinks and hot mauves in an exuberant display of brilliant color.

ABOVE: In a frenzy of color, texture, and shape, this balcony scene demands attention. Among the many elements are black-eyed Susans (*Rudbeckia hirta*), sunflowers (*Helianthus* spp.), marigolds (*Tagetes* spp.), dahlias, and nasturtiums (*Tropaeolum majus*) in bold shades of gold and yellow. Single red dahlias with a unifying gold center are a welcome embellishment and highlight the surprise of ripening cherry tomatoes. Growing plants in containers gives the gardener wonderful flexibility to experiment with whimsical and unusual elements.

OPPOSITE: A collection of yellow and gold blooms with traces of umber unite in a monochromatic vignette in the corner of a stone terrace. At the center is an elegantly elongated calla lily trumpet of an unusual shade of gold with orange marbling. The colors are repeated in the surrounding gazania, marigold, chrysanthemum, and *Rudbeckia*. A bit of variegated leaf, including the calla's white speckles and the silvery undersides of the gazania's leaf, adds a ripple of excitement.

ABOVE: Cascading tuberous begonias in an animated shade of tangerine contrast vividly with delicate purple lobelia blooms. Such a combination might seem a bit jarring for those who favor subtlety, but it is certainly appropriate when strong contrasts and an adamant visual statement are called for.

LEFT: The thick, leathery texture of agave spikes contrasts sharply with the thin, almost papery disks of nasturtium foliage. Texture is a design element that is often overlooked, especially by the novice gardener. There is no shortage of diversity in plant textures. Consider the suede-like oxalis, velvety lambs ears and pansies, succulent sedums, crisp strawflowers, waxy bergenia, nubbly yarrow, and quilted hostas, which demonstrate but a few of the plant world's many textures.

OPPOSITE: The cherry red of old-fashioned wax begonias comes with built-in contrast in the form of yellow eyes and shiny deep maroon leaves. In this vignette, variegated ivy and a gray stone terrace surround the begonia, setting off beautifully the warm tones of the flowers and foliage.

ABOVE: The rich bronze colors of autumn are at their peak in this handsome grouping of containers. A young Japanese maple (*Acer palmatum*) forms a canopy of gold-tinged burgundy over pots of sedum, black-eyed Susans (*Rudbeckia hirta*), heather (*Calluna* spp.), Japanese blood grass (*Imperata cylindrica* var. *rubra*), firethorn (*Pyracantha coccinea*), flowering kale, and ornamental grasses crowded below. Containers allow the gardener freedom to tailor a display to the season.

ABOVE LEFT: When working with pots, make sure to give careful consideration to proportion. Here, exquisite cobalt blue glazed pots in two sizes house perky gold calendula with spikes of cordyline adding needed height to the larger container. Shorter dracena spikes have the same effect in the smaller pot.

OPPOSITE: A hanging basket is barely able to contain the exuberant growth of petunias, impatiens, and two varieties of fuchsia. Though the combination appears at first glance to be a simple grouping of lively color, a closer examination reveals the efforts of a skilled designer. Note the way the red of the impatiens mimics the red of the two-toned fuchsia, while the lavender-pink petunias appear as a prelude to the shades found in the fading fuchsia's blooms.